948.
02

History in Evidence

VIKING BRITAIN

Tony D. Triggs

Wayland

History in Evidence
Medieval Britain
Norman Britain
Prehistoric Britain
Roman Britain
Saxon Britain
Tudor Britain
Victorian Britain
Viking Britain

Cover design: Alison Anholt-White
Series design: Helen White
Consultant: Dr Margaret L Faull

Cover pictures: The main picture shows the Viking
church at Birsay, Orkney. The inset is a chess piece
found on the Isle of Lewis, Scotland.

First published in 1989 by
Wayland (Publishers) Limited
61 Western Road, Hove
East Sussex BN3 1JD, England

British Library Cataloguing in Publication Data
Triggs, Tony D.
  Viking Britain.
  1. Great Britain, Vikings. Social life
  I. Title II. Series
  941.01

HARDBACK ISBN 1–85210–577–1

PAPERBACK ISBN 0–7502–0529–6

Edited and typeset by Kudos, Hove, East Sussex
Printed in Italy by G. Canale & C.S.p.A., Turin
Bound in France by A.G.M.

Picture acknowledgements
The author would like to thank Linda James and the
York Archaeological Trust for their help in the
preparation of this book. The publishers wish to thank
the following for permission to reproduce their
illustrations on the pages mentioned: C M Dixon/
Photoresources *cover* (inset), 11 (left), 18 (lower);
Werner Forman Archive 11 (right); Michael Holford
10, 20; Dr Anna Ritchie 8, 9; Royal Museum of
Scotland 21 (upper); Ronald Sheridan/The Ancient Art
& Architecture Collection *cover* (main picture), 7, 28;
TOPHAM 30; Yorkshire Archaeological Trust 12, 13
(both), 14, 15, 16, 17, 18 (upper), 21 (lower), 24 (both),
25, 26, 27 (both), 29. The artwork was supplied by the
following: Malcolm S Walker 4, 5; Stephen Wheele 7.

Contents

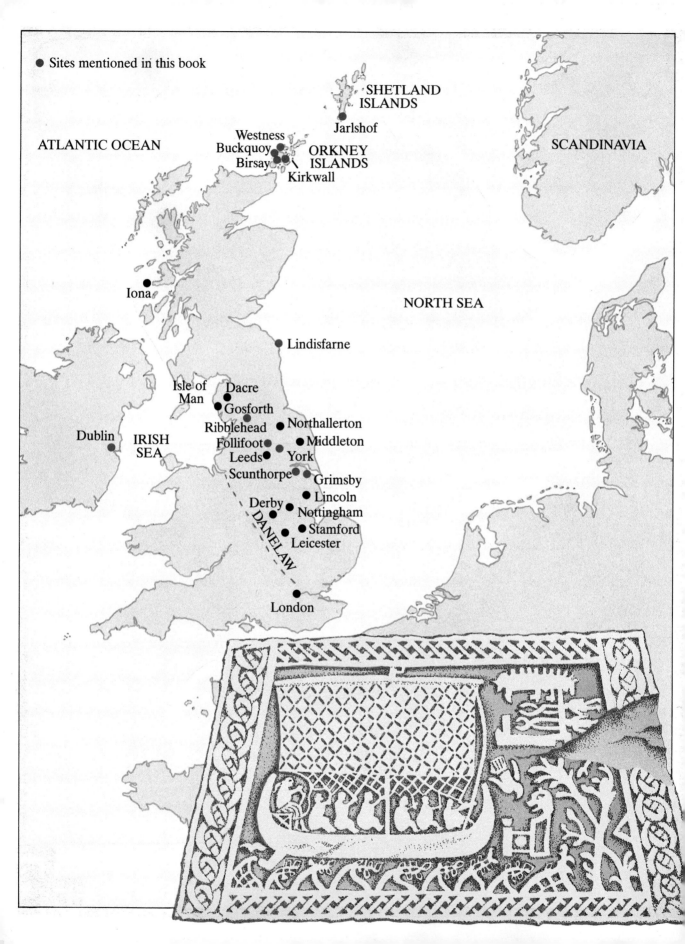

Who were the Vikings?

'Save us, Lord, from the fury of the Northmen.' For several centuries this prayer was said all over Europe, for the Northmen, or Vikings, were raiding and conquering much of the continent. They came from Scandinavia, and the English and Scots were among their victims.

There are all sorts of clues about the Vikings, and the things that people wrote at the time – or left unfinished – are very important. Archaeologists also find things the Vikings made and used, and sometimes they even find their boats.

Recently, people have tried building copies of Viking boats, and some have been sailed on rivers in Britain. In earlier times, the sight of a Viking boat would have sent people running for safety. We know of their fear because some church towers have doorways well above the ground. Local people must have used the towers as hide-outs during Viking attacks. They probably got inside by climbing ladders which they drew up behind them.

OPPOSITE This map shows where the Vikings came from and the main towns and cities of Viking Britain (the area called Danelaw). The picture at the bottom is a copy of a stone carving of Viking boats coming across the North Sea to raid Britain.

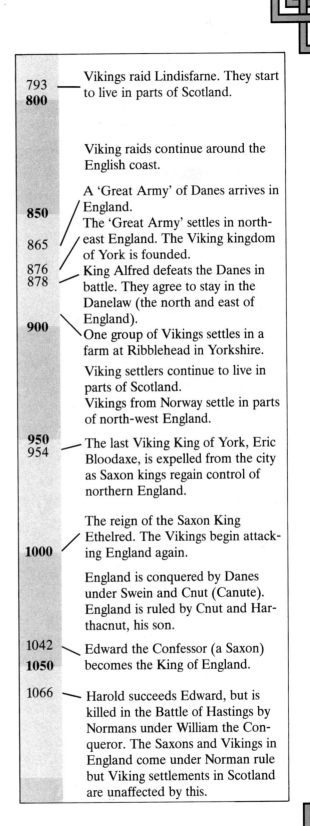

793 **800**	Vikings raid Lindisfarne. They start to live in parts of Scotland.
	Viking raids continue around the English coast.
850	A 'Great Army' of Danes arrives in England.
865	The 'Great Army' settles in north-east England. The Viking kingdom of York is founded.
876 878	King Alfred defeats the Danes in battle. They agree to stay in the Danelaw (the north and east of England).
900	One group of Vikings settles in a farm at Ribblehead in Yorkshire.
	Viking settlers continue to live in parts of Scotland. Vikings from Norway settle in parts of north-west England.
950 954	The last Viking King of York, Eric Bloodaxe, is expelled from the city as Saxon kings regain control of northern England.
1000	The reign of the Saxon King Ethelred. The Vikings begin attacking England again.
	England is conquered by Danes under Swein and Cnut (Canute). England is ruled by Cnut and Harthacnut, his son.
1042 **1050**	Edward the Confessor (a Saxon) becomes the King of England.
1066	Harold succeeds Edward, but is killed in the Battle of Hastings by Normans under William the Conqueror. The Saxons and Vikings in England come under Norman rule but Viking settlements in Scotland are unaffected by this.

5

Living on a farm

Most of the Vikings who settled in Britain lived by farming. Sometimes archaeologists find the remains of a Viking farm. One was found at Ribblehead in North Yorkshire. Patterns of mounds and boulders on a grassy hilltop showed where Viking buildings had stood 1,000 years ago. The walls of the biggest building had been up to 3 m thick, and the Vikings had made them from boulders, chunks of rock and soil.

Because of its size, the archaeologists guessed that the biggest building had been a farmhouse. When they removed the grass that had grown there, they found a spearhead and several knives. It seemed that animals had been killed in the open, then dragged to the farmhouse to be cut up and cooked. The floor of the farmhouse was made of earth, and the Vikings cooked their food on an open fire. The fire also kept them warm and gave them light. This was important, for the house did not have any windows.

The farm was built on very high ground, so the weather must have been stormy in winter. The thick walls helped to keep the family snug and warm, but what was the roof like? The archaeologists studied the chunks of rock that the Vikings had used for the walls. They found that some of them had deep pits and they guessed that these had held posts to support a thatched roof. Thatch lets smoke through, but rain

Place names
We know where the Vikings built their farms because the places still have Viking names. Names that end with 'by' and 'thorpe' were nearly all given by Viking settlers. Whitby began when a Viking called Hviti started farming there. A 'thorpe' was a smaller farm or settlement built when a larger one needed new land. Scunthorpe, in Lincolnshire, was founded by a Viking called Skuma.

runs off it as long as it has a steep enough slope. Although the building did not have an upstairs, it must have been tall.

Some of the patterns on the hilltops showed where sheep had been kept in the winter. However, one shape marked a special building. The archaeologists cleared away the grass and they found a burnt patch and some traces of iron. This showed where a smith had once worked. They also found part of a spindle used for spinning thread. The Vikings made nearly all the things they needed, including tools and cloth.

OPPOSITE The farm at Ribblehead. As well as the main house, there was a kitchen (right) and a workshop. The photograph in the top left corner shows the remains of houses at the Brough of Birsay, Orkney.

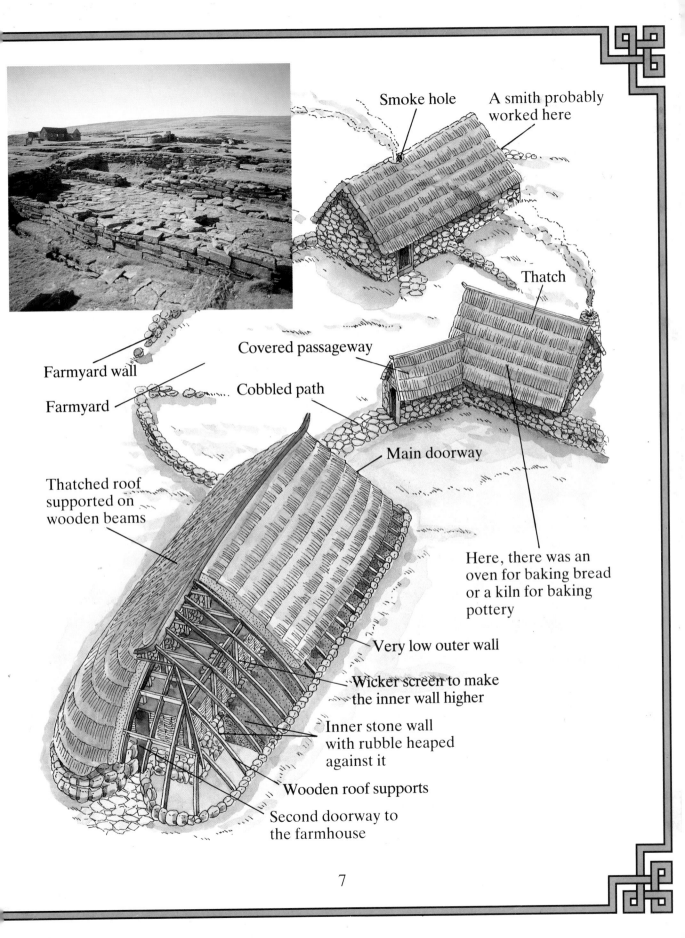

Smoke hole

A smith probably worked here

Thatch

Covered passageway

Farmyard wall

Farmyard

Cobbled path

Main doorway

Thatched roof supported on wooden beams

Here, there was an oven for baking bread or a kiln for baking pottery

Very low outer wall

Wicker screen to make the inner wall higher

Inner stone wall with rubble heaped against it

Wooden roof supports

Second doorway to the farmhouse

A farm in Scotland

Vikings settled in many parts of Scotland. One of the places they chose was Buckquoy, in the Orkney Islands. Buckquoy is the Old Norse (or Viking) name for a barley field, and this shows that barley was one of their crops.

Archaeologists have found the remains of some Viking buildings at Buckquoy. They were like the buildings at Ribblehead, but the archaeologists found many extra clues about the Vikings' diet and way of life. For example, they found about 2,000 bones. Most of them came from cattle, sheep and pigs, but some came from horses, goats and deer. There were also fish-bones and various shells. We know that the Scottish Vikings were expert fishermen. Some Viking boats had knobs where the fishermen tied their line, and archaeologists have found the

Excavating the remains of a ninth-century house at Buckquoy, on the Orkney Islands.

Grass growing over the foundations of a Viking house at the Brough of Birsay, Orkney.

remains of a Viking boathouse at a place called Westness in the Orkneys.

One of the buildings at Buckquoy had a stone gutter in the middle of the floor. The gutter was clogged with a sort of sludge and a sample was sent to be tested in a laboratory. The scientists found that the sample had chemicals normally found in urine and dung. They wondered whether the building had been a cattle shed or a toilet for humans, so they studied the sample through a microscope. It contained bits of grass which had been through an animal's stomach, so it had probably been a cattle shed.

The archaeologists soon found another 'mystery building'. It was strange because it faced south-west, and the wind in the Orkneys usually blows from that direction. The Vikings did not like their buildings to face straight into the wind, which encouraged draughts and damaged roofs. The building was also unusual because it had a stone floor. (The Vikings usually made do with earth floors.) Perhaps the building was used for threshing grain crops, like barley. Threshing could only be done if the floor was hard and smooth, and a breeze would be needed to blow away the chaff. The front and the back of the building were probably open to let the wind blow through.

9

Religion

ABOVE A well-preserved example of an eleventh-century Viking grave stone. It was excavated at St Paul's Cathedral, in London. It shows a lion fighting a giant snake.

When the Vikings came to Britain, they were pagans. Their gods included Odin, Thor, Freyr and Tiu, and the land of the gods was know as Asgard. There was also a race of evil giants who lived in a stony wasteland called Utgard.

Odin was the king of the gods, and he ruled over wisdom, farming and war. Warriors who were killed in battle went to live in his feasting hall, which was called Valhalla. They were led there by Odin's servants, known as Valkyries, who rode to battlefields and chose which warriors would die. In Valhalla, the Valkyries gave

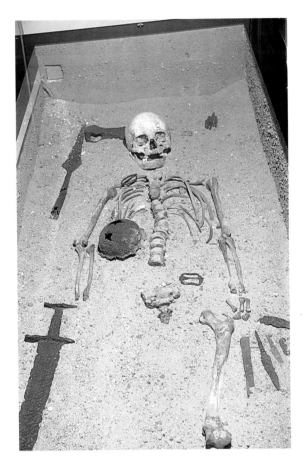

At Buckquoy, archaeologists found the skeleton of a newly born baby buried in the floor of a farmhouse. The body had been taken to pieces, and some people think the baby had been killed and buried as part of a ritual. Perhaps the house was new and the Vikings were asking the gods to save them from storms and bad luck.

By the tenth century, the Vikings had become Christians. We know this from various clues. For example, we find Viking graves in Christian graveyards and Viking designs on Christian crosses. The Vikings even built their own churches. They built a church and perhaps a bishop's palace at Birsay in the Orkney Islands, as well as a cathedral at Kirkwall.

ABOVE A Viking warrior would have been buried in this way, with his axe, spear, sword, knives, shield, belt (only the buckle remains) and arrows (only the metal heads remain).

them drinks in their enemies' skulls.

The Vikings tried to please the gods by saying prayers and making sacrifices. We know about this from things they wrote. For example, in a poem called *Ynglinga Saga*, a Viking explained: 'Freyr is beautiful and powerful. He makes the rain and sunshine and has power over all that grows in the ground. It is well to pray to him for good seasons and peace.'

This is St Magnus Cathedral, Kirkwall, Orkney, which was begun in 1137.

Digging up a street

Many Vikings lived in towns and cities, such as Dublin and York, but modern buildings often prevent archaeologists from digging up clues about their lives. However, in 1966 and 1970, York City Council bought some disused buildings in a street known as Coppergate. They said that they would demolish the buildings and let archaeologists look for remains of earlier buildings underneath. The archaeologists started work in 1976. They soon found the stumps of wooden fence-posts, which showed that the Vikings had divided the site into four narrow plots. The plots ran right from the street to the nearby River Foss, and some people think the Viking owners used the river to bring supplies.

At the front of each plot, the Vikings dug rectangular pits as big as cellars. After digging the pits, they lined them with enormous planks, which were held in place with wooden posts. The archaeologists wanted to find out what the pits

This path was discovered during excavations at York. The surface was rough, so it stopped the Vikings slipping in the mud.

were for, so they carefully cleared out all the soil that had fallen into them. At last they came to the earth floor which the Vikings had used. They found clues, such as food remains, which showed that Vikings had lived in the pits. The tops of the walls had disappeared, but they must have risen above ground level or the Vikings could never have stood up straight.

The buildings probably had thatched roofs, but because they were set so low in the ground they must have looked like rows of tents.

The archaeologists wondered how people had got in and out of the houses. Had they been forced to use ladders and trap-doors? The answer was found at the back of the houses. The Vikings had dug deep trenches leading down to their homes. These trenches must have been passageways, and they led to gaps in the wooden walls. We cannot be sure if the houses had doors, and this is a question the archaeologists still have to solve.

Excavating all that remains of Jorvik, the Viking name for York. It was the capital of northern England and a large port.

Some of the houses at Jorvik were in deep pits which were lined with enormous planks, held in place with wooden posts.

More clues in the ground

Archaeologists carefully excavating the remains in York of buildings made of wattle and clay. These buildings were older than the Vikings' sunken houses.

The sunken houses were not the first Viking buildings in Coppergate. The archaeologists found the remains of earlier buildings. The walls were made of wattle (upright stakes with long straight branches woven between them). There were pieces of hardened clay in the soil, and the clay had patterns that had come from the branches. The Vikings had probably coated the walls with clay to stop draughts. Some people think that they may have hung cloth or animal skins on the inside too.

They certainly used to have blazing fires. We know this because huge hearths have been found. Even then, these houses may have been too cool and draughty, so perhaps this is why the Vikings replaced them.

There were various clues which showed

14

which houses had been built first. For example, parts of the wattle houses had been destroyed when the Vikings built their sunken homes. Secondly, coins were found in the floors and the archaeologists knew the dates when they had been minted. Lastly, the archaeologists used a method called dendrochronology, or tree-ring dating. All these methods of dating showed that the wattle houses had been built first.

Once the archaeologists had found out all they could, a museum, called the Jorvik Centre, was built on the site. Jorvik is the Viking name for York, and people who go there can see the remains of the Viking buildings. They can also see full-size models of them just as they were in Viking times, with Vikings sitting round their fires or doing jobs like spinning and weaving. Visitors go round the exhibition in 'Time Cars'. The sounds and smells of Viking life are included, and many visitors feel that they are Vikings, sharing the life of a city 1,000 years ago.

Dendrochronology
Trees grow at different speeds according to the weather. A pattern of rings can be seen in the wood, showing how much a tree has grown each year. Archaeologists can compare the pattern on a newly found piece of wood with the pattern on pieces whose dates they know. If the patterns match, then the date is the same.

In Jorvik, narrow alleys like this one led to the backs of houses and down to the river.

Cesspits and wells

Archaeologists often find pits near Viking workshops and houses. Most were probably rubbish pits, but some were used as cesspits (toilets) and others were used as store-rooms and wells. The Vikings sometimes lined their wells with wood to keep the water clean. The storage pits were usually lined with basketwork. This was enough to stop the soil from caving in, and the moist, cool conditions helped to preserve important supplies, such as leather and grain.

Several pits were found behind the houses in Coppergate. Some contained the Vikings' rubbish. This included animals' bones and all sorts of broken and worn-out possessions. The archaeologists also found a number of cesspits. One contained a wooden board with a hole in the middle. The Vikings probably put it across the pit and used it as a toilet seat. In another cesspit, the archaeologists found a wickerwork screen. This had probably stood around the cesspit to give people privacy when they used it.

The cesspits were full of coprolites. Coprolites are lumps of excrement (dung), and some sorts of soil can preserve them for many hundreds of years. The archaeologists studied them under microscopes to find out about the Vikings' diet. As well as meat, the Vikings at York ate food made from grain crops, like wheat and oats. The wheat was probably ground into flour and baked in loaves; the oats were probably made into porridge.

A lump of human excrement, which was found in one of the cesspits excavated by archaeologists in York. When studied under a microscope in a laboratory, it can tell us about the Vikings' diet and illnesses. We know that the Vikings ate corncockle seeds, which would have given them upset stomachs. Tiny eggs from worms in their stomachs have also been found in Vikings' excrement. The worms came from dirty drinking water.

ABOVE This display at the Jorvik Centre shows what a toilet would have been like. Toilets (holes in the earth) were just outside the houses and surrounded by a wickerwork fence to give the occupant some privacy from his or her neighbours.

The coprolites contained bits of corn-cockle seed that had got mixed up with the Vikings' grain. Corncockle seeds are poisonous, so the Vikings must have suffered from stomach aches and diarrhoea. The coprolites also contained tiny eggs from worms that lived in the Vikings' stomachs. The Vikings' toilets and wells were rather close together, and germs and parasites' eggs from the toilets could easily enter the drinking water. The Vikings had lined their wells to keep the water clean, but they did not understand about things too small to see.

Fun and games

The Vikings had all sorts of pastimes, and music was one of the things they liked best. Skilful craftsmen made instruments, such as lyres (small harps), but poorer people made simple instruments for themselves. Children made whistles from the leg-bones of birds. The bones were hollow and the children just had to chip some holes along a bone to get different notes.

The Vikings had various outdoor activities. Heavy balls have been found, which some people think were used by the Vikings to play a game like bowls. A number of ice-skates have also been discovered, but we cannot be sure that the

ABOVE A horse shoe, which was excavated by archaeologists in York.

These chess pieces were discovered on the Isle of Lewis, Scotland. They are made of walrus tusks and they date from about 1140.

The Vikings enjoyed playing board games during the long, cold winter evenings. This game is called *Hnefatafl*. The pieces belonged to a Viking family, but the board is a modern one.

Vikings ever skated for pleasure. Perhaps they used skates to get across frozen lakes or rivers in winter.

The Vikings loved riding. We know this because there are several places in north-east England called Hesketh or Hesket, and these names come from the Viking words meaning 'horse-race' or 'horse-track'. There is also a place called Follifoot, and this means 'horse-fight'. It seems that the Vikings sometimes goaded horses and other animals to fight each other. Perhaps they gambled on which animal would win.

The Vikings spent their winter evenings playing board games. Dice, counters and boards have been found at many sites in Britain.

Horse fights
A Viking poem helps to confirm that this cruel sport really did take place. The poem, called *Njal's Saga*, says that two fighting horses 'went at each other and bit each other for a very long time without having to be goaded on.'

Clothes and jewels

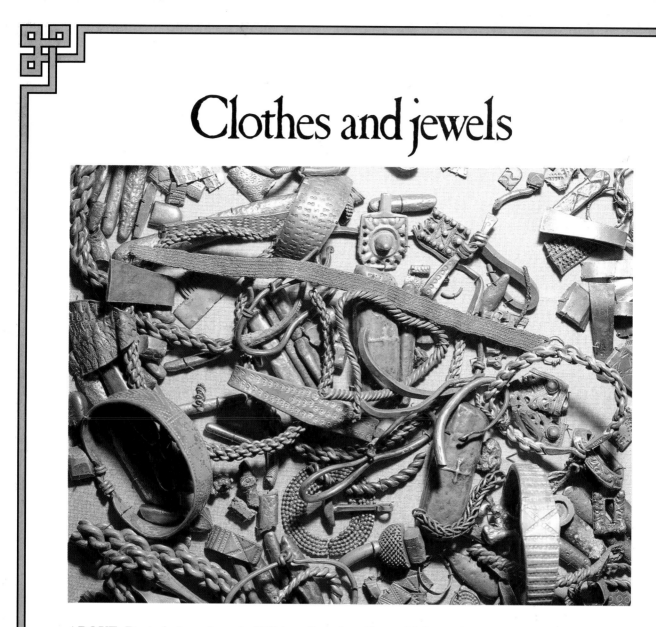

ABOVE Part of a huge hoard of Viking silver jewellery which was found in a chest on the banks of the River Ribble in Lancashire in 1840. Archaeologists think that most of the pieces were made around 900. This is the largest Viking treasure ever discovered in Europe.

We know about the Vikings' clothing in various ways. Some of our information comes from carvings, pictures and things people wrote. *Njal's Saga* tells of a woman 'dressed in a cloak of blue woven material. Beneath it she had a scarlet skirt with a silver belt.' The same poem mentions a man who was 'wearing a blue tunic with a silver belt, blue striped trousers and black boots.'

Clues about Viking clothes are also found in the soil. The poem mentioned woven material, and at Buckquoy archaeologists have found clay rings which were used to weight spindles and keep them spinning as long as possible. At other sites they have found the remains of some weaving looms.

Many sheep bones are found at Viking farms, and the Vikings made their cloth from the wool. The rough woollen cloth must have made them itch, but the richer Vikings solved this problem by wearing linen underclothes. Linen is made from a plant called flax, and flax seeds are sometimes found in the soil at Viking sites. Archaeologists also find the remains of plants that were used to dye the cloth. A plant called weld gave a yellow dye, while woad gave a blue dye and madder turned things bright red. Some of the clothes mentioned in *Njal's Saga* had probably been dyed with woad.

Leather and cloth usually rot away in the soil, but some sorts of soil preserve things well. At York, archaeologists found a number of leather shoes. They also found some worn-out soles, which the Vikings must have thrown away. The peaty soil in Danish bogs has preserved the bodies of several Vikings, including their clothes.

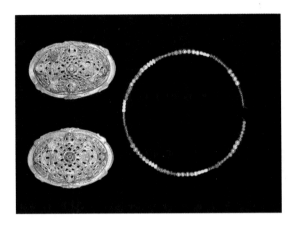

ABOVE These beautiful brooches were used by a woman to fasten her cloak.

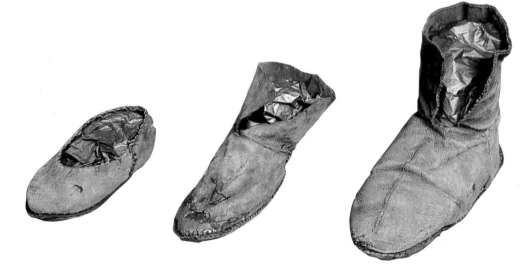

Leather boots and a shoe, which were unearthed in excavations at York. Leather survives well in damp soil, whereas in dry earth it will rot away.

Food and drink

The Vikings enjoyed a wide range of foods, but the choice depended on where people lived and how rich they were. A Viking poem mentions 'Coarse bread that was thick and heavy and full of husks.' It also talks about 'fine white bread that was made from wheat', but this was served at a banquet for someone very rich.

We know that the Vikings grew other grain crops as well as wheat. The name Buckquoy gives us a clue to this, and clues have also been found in the soil. At Westness, in the Orkney Islands, archaeologists found grains of barley and rye. They also studied the soil with microscopes and they found tiny specks of pollen which had come from oats.

All sorts of pips and seeds have been found at Viking sites. They show that the Vikings ate apples, plums, berries and nuts. They also ate vegetables, including cabbages, carrots and parsnips.

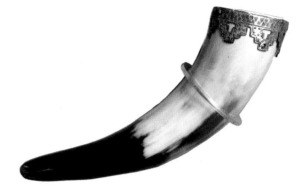

ABOVE A drinking horn, which was probably used for mead at meal-times.

The Vikings had never heard of sugar. They sweetened their food and drink with honey, and they used it to make a strong drink, called mead. Viking poems often mentioned mead, and archaeologists found the remains of a beehive at York. The Vikings also drank lots of milk, and some was turned into butter and cheese.

In cities, people often bought live animals, then killed them in their own backyards. We know this because the skulls are sometimes found there in pieces. This shows how the Vikings killed the animals; it also suggests that they did it where the skulls are found. If they had killed them outside the city they would have left the skulls behind.

At Jarlshof, in the Shetland Islands, archaeologists have found the remains of a stone oven, and it seems that the Vikings cooked their food by adding hot pebbles.

A wooden cup and bowl, which were found in the excavations of Viking York.

They also cooked things in cauldrons over blazing fires. Lastly, they sometimes put chunks of meat or fish on wooden or metal spits and held them in the flames. The wooden spits have not survived but metal ones have been found at many Viking sites. (The words 'steak' and 'stick'

ABOVE   A pottery storage jar which was also found at York.

are connected because a steak was a piece of meat the Vikings cooked on a stick. Even our language gives us clues about Viking life.)

Coins and trade

ABOVE The die (right) was used to imprint designs on coins. It was tested on the piece of lead at the top of the picture .

Thousands of Viking coins have been found in Britain and other Viking lands. Some of the coins were made of bronze, and examples of these were found at Ribblehead. Others, made of silver, have been discovered at sites throughout England and Scotland.

To make coins, a Viking craftsman needed a hammer and a pair of dies (blocks of metal for stamping designs). He put a round piece of bronze or silver between his dies and brought the hammer down on them sharply. This stamped the designs on the metal disc and turned it into a proper coin.

The Vikings were keen to trade with their neighbours. They also traded with people who lived in distant lands. Archaeologists often find things which had been carried hundreds of kilometres by ship or on horseback.

Amber (hardened sap from trees) was one of the things which Viking sailors brought to Britain. Most of the amber came from northern Europe, and archaeologists can sometimes prove this by examining insects caught inside it. The Vikings carved the amber into all sorts of

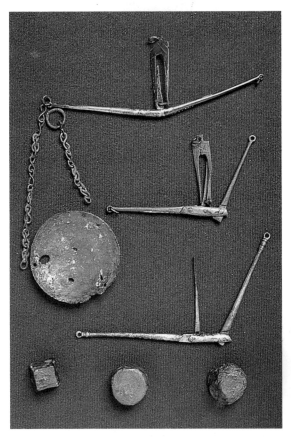

A merchant would have used these folding scales to check the coins his customers gave him when buying goods.

objects, such as beads, rings and even chessmen. They exported some of their finished work, and amber jewellery made in Britain is found in Europe.

A lost purse gave archaeologists another clue about Viking trade. A Viking lost it in Ireland in 925 and archaeologists found it there. They could tell from coins inside the purse that the Viking was on a visit from England. However, a few of the coins in the purse had been made at Samarkand in Asia. This showed that Vikings from England did not just trade with their cousins in Ireland and northern Europe; they also traded with people in faraway parts of the world. Traces of silk from Samarkand have been found at a number of Viking sites too.

Furs and skins, whalebone, pottery, wine and stone were brought to England from all over Europe. Some of the stone was used to make millstones. The Vikings in Britain grew plenty of grain but they had to import the rough stone needed for grinding it up. They did not use all the grain themselves, for Viking poems say that they sent supplies to Iceland, where bad weather sometimes ruined crops.

Merchants carried folding scales and used them to check the coins they were given. This was important, for the coin-makers might try to cheat by using the wrong sort of metal or making the coins too thin and light. Several forged and underweight coins have been found in places where Vikings lived.

This amber necklace was made by a jeweller in Jorvik. The amber came from abroad.

Working with wood

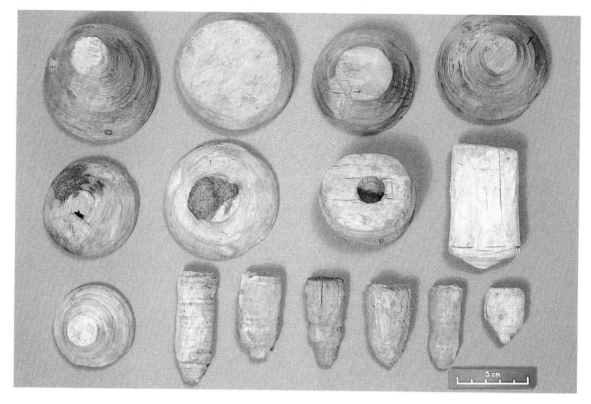

ABOVE These unwanted cores were thrown away by a man who made wooden bowls and cups in Jorvik. Coppergate, or Cup Street, probably got its name because of the work done there.

The archaeologists who worked in York wanted to know how Coppergate got its name. They knew it came from the Viking words for 'cup' and 'street', but why should the Vikings call it Cup Street?

Soon they began to find clues in the soil. Someone discovered a small wooden knob, and many similar knobs were found as the work went on. It became clear that a Viking had thrown them away in his rubbish. Each sunken house had a work-

shop behind it, and one belonged to a man who made wooden cups. He gave each cup a smooth round shape, then hollowed it out and, as he did so, a useless core was cut away. The archaeologists had found these cores. They had also found why the street was called Cup Street, or Coppergate, and they realised that it had been very busy, with lots of noisy buying and selling. The cup-maker probably sold his cups in front of his house. His neighbour

ABOVE These metal tools were used by the cup-maker in his workshop in Coppergate and were found by archaeologists one thousand years later.

At the Jorvik Centre in York, you can see a display showing the cup-maker at work.

made metal goods and jewellery, and he must have had a little stall too. Perhaps the other residents also had small businesses.

The Vikings made their cups and bowls from pottery as well as wood. Some bowls were also cut from stone. At Cunningsburgh, in the Shetland Islands, the Vikings quarried a soft sort of stone, called steatite or soapstone. They did not carry the stone away to distant workshops. Instead, they made the bowls on the spot. They simply chiselled them out of the stone, and some half-finished bowls can still be seen at the quarry today. They are fixed to the stone because the craftsmen never cut them away. However, several finished bowls have been found at Jarlshof, in the Shetlands.

Weapons and war

Viking warriors were very attached to their swords and often gave them nick-names. Some warriors had their swords buried with them when they died; others left them to their sons.

They saw King Magnus's fleet bearing down on them, and saw too that in front of the fleet the sea looked as it does in heavy rain in still weather. This shower came quickly on, and it was arrow fall. Then shields were needed. This description comes from a Viking poem and it reminds us that the Vikings were expert archers. It also shows that they used shields to protect themselves.

The Vikings often put people's belongings in their graves. Perhaps they thought that the owners would want to use them in another life. Some Viking graves contain small groups of arrow-heads. The wooden shafts have rotted away, but the metal heads are often found in perfect condition. Axe-heads, spear-heads and swords are also found in graves.

Swords were the Vikings' favourite weapon, and many were up to a metre long. The blades were made in a special way to give them strength and stop them from snapping. The smith took several strips of iron and heated them up till they joined together. Before they hardened, he bent them into a spiral shape, then he flattened it out and welded the steel cutting edges in place. Other craftsmen finished the sword by fitting a hilt. Some hilts were made of bone or ivory and many had jewels on the end.

Swords were so precious that fathers passed them on to their sons, like family treasures. The Vikings even gave their swords names. One Viking sword was known as 'Leg-biter' and another was known as 'Gleam of Battle'.

Because of the way in which they were made, Viking swords had patterns like the

This helmet was found in 1982 during the building of the Jorvik Centre. However, archaeologists do not think it belonged to a Viking. They say it was probably worn by a powerful Anglo-Saxon lord during the battle for York in 866. The helmet was not in a very good condition when it was discovered, but it was carefully repaired and restored to go on display in the Centre.

skin of a snake. Some Vikings thought that the pattern was magical. They tried to add extra magic by inscribing swords with mysterious letters, known as runes.

Sword blades often had a groove running down each side. The groove saved metal and made the sword lighter. It also made it more deadly, since a victim's blood could flow along the groove while the sword was stuck into him. Because of this, the groove is sometimes known as the 'blood channel'.

Many carvings and pictures show Viking weapons. In 1066, the Normans, who were cousins of the Vikings, crossed the English Channel and defeated the British in battle. Later, a group of women embroidered a huge comic strip, called the *Bayeux Tapestry*. It tells the story of the battle and shows us the sorts of weapon the Vikings and Normans used when fighting each other.

Places to visit

Cambridge: Museum of Archaeology and Ethnology

Douglas, Isle of Man: Manx Museum and Art Gallery

Dublin: National Museum of Ireland

Edinburgh: National Museum of Antiquities of Scotland

Kirkwall, Orkney: Tankerness House Museum

London: British Museum

Newcastle-upon-Tyne: Museum of Antiquities of the University and the Society of Antiquaries of Newcastle-upon-Tyne

Oxford: Ashmolean Museum

Sumburgh Head, Shetland: Jarlshof

York: Castle Museum, Jorvik Viking Centre, Yorkshire Museum

Bayeux Tapestry

This is on display at Bayeux in France, but the following British museums have copies of it: Reading Museum and Art Gallery (an embroidered copy); the Victoria and Albert Museum, London (photographic copy). In each case, it is advisable to check that the tapestry will be on show.

Young Archaeologists Club

If you are interested in finding out more about archaeology, you might like to join this club. Further information can be obtained from: Young Archaeologists Club, United House, Piccadilly, York YO1 1PQ.

BELOW Some 'modern' Viking warriors re-enacting a battle outside York.

Glossary

Archaeologist A person who studies ancient remains found in the ground or underwater.

Basketwork *See* wickerwork below.

Boulder A large stone.

Cauldron A large cooking pot.

Chaff The unwanted bits of corn separated in threshing.

Diet People's food and drink.

Export To send goods abroad to be sold; the opposite of import (see below).

Flax A plant whose seeds are crushed to make linseed oil. Fibres from its stems were used by the Vikings to make linen cloth.

Forge To copy something to deceive people into thinking it is the real thing.

Goad To make a person or an animal angry on purpose.

Gutter A long, narrow channel at the side of a street that carries away dirty water.

Heathen *See* pagans below.

Import To buy goods from another country.

Mint To make coins.

Pagans People who worship many gods.

Smith Someone who makes things out of metal: for example, a blacksmith makes things out of iron and a silversmith makes things out of silver.

Thresh To beat corn to get the grain (seeds) out of it.

Trapdoor A door in a ceiling, roof or floor.

Wickerwork Things made out of reeds or canes which have been woven together.

Books to read

Clarke, H. *A Closer Look at Vikings* (Hamish Hamilton, 1979)

Ferguson, S. *Growing Up in Viking Times* (Batsford, 1971)

George, S. *The Vikings* (David & Charles, 1976)

Gibb, C. *A Viking Sailor* (Wayland, 1982)

Gibson, M. *The Vikings* (Macdonald Educational, 1976)

Gibson, M. *The Vikings* (Wayland, 1987)

Magnusson, M. *Vikings!* (Bodley Head, 1973)

Place, R. *The Vikings* (Longman, 1980)

Place, R. *The Vikings: Fact and Fiction* (Cambridge University Press, 1985)

Simpson, J. *Everyday Life in the Viking Age* (Batsford, 1967)

Index